INTRODUCTION TO ISLAMIC CREED

Say, [O Prophet], "He is Allah—One [and Indivisible];
Allah—the Sustainer [needed by all].
He has never had offspring, nor was He born.
And there is none comparable to Him."

SURAH AL-IKHLAS

رسالة في علم التوحيد

INTRODUCTION TO ISLAMIC CREED
Risālat fi 'Ilm al-Tawhīd

Compiled by
Imam Ibrahim al-Bajuri

Translation & Notes by
Rashad Jameer

Questions may be directed to publishing@imamghazali.org.

Title: Introduction to Islamic Creed
ISBN: 978-0-692-71042-5
Fourth Print – December 2019

Note: Page numbering differs between the fourth print and previous prints.
Author: Imam Ibrahim al-Bajuri
Translator: Rashad Jameer ◆ www.wasilapress.com
Proofreader: Abdul Aziz Suraqah
Cover Designer: Ahmed Osman ◆ info@ahmedosman.com.au
Typesetter: Imran Rahim ◆ enquiries@ethereadesign.com
Islamic Calligraphy: Courtesy of The Prince Ghazi Trust

Stock or custom editions of titles may be purchased in bulk for educational, business, fundraising, or sales promotional use. For more information or to contact a representative of Imam Ghazali Publishing, please contact publishing@imamghazali.org.

Book One — Media Access

IGI ESSENTIALS SERIES

This book comes with access to an exclusive media library to study the text with a teacher.

www.islamiccreed.org
Promo code: HUYSGHDYUIG4

Contents

Foreword

Islamic theology has always been an area of great interest and richness since Muslims moved from the Arabian Peninsula to mix with people who had inherited a rich and heavy amount of theological questions. Even though *kalam* developed as a response to new situations that required Islam to give its view on various, more intricate and complicated questions, an average Muslim is not required to get involved in those academic debates that require long reading and a sophisticated mentality. However, every Muslim is required to strengthen his faith and free himself from the bondage of blind imitation by knowing some simple proofs that allow the tenets of his belief to make sense to him, otherwise, he may fall into the trap of doubts and confusion.

In their attempt to make the tenets of belief easy and understandable to the average Muslim, scholars have written simple expositions of Islamic belief that suit any individual who is willing to know what he should really believe in. One of these scholars is the great *Shaykh al-Islam Burhan al-Din* al-Bajuri, who assumed the leadership and Sheikhdom of the Grand al-Azhar Mosque in Cairo, and was a prolific writer and a great teacher. Imam al-Bajuri was born in the northern Delta governorate al-Munufiyyah 1198 AH – 1783 CE and started his studies in al-Azhar in 1213 AH – 1797 CE under great luminaries like Imam Muhammad al-Amir and Shaykh Muhammad al-Fadali. His writings include his marginalia on *Jawharah al-Tawhid*, his marginalia on the *al-Sullam* in logic and his marginalia on the *al-Burdah* poem. His works are characterized by depth and have been received with great acceptance by circles of Islamic scholarship.

Our dear brother and student, Ustadh Rashad Jameer, has been successful in choosing a simple, but essential work of Imam al-Bajuri to make available in English. Since a good choice is a sign of good endings, as Ibn 'Ata Illah hints when he says, '*burning starts lead to shining ends*,' I pray that Allah puts immense benefit in this book as a primary text for Muslims in the West to learn the essentials of Islamic creed. More advanced students may find it beneficial to look into larger works. While it is highly recommended to look into our heritage and learn it, Islamic theology needs great efforts to add to its topics the modern theological questions that need to be answered to make it more relatable and to contextualize its debates and discussions.

I pray that this book is a start of many in this important area, and thank the translator for his efforts in the service of this great cause of Sacred Knowledge. Success is from Almighty Allah.

AHMED SAAD AL-AZHARI AL-HASANI
Ihsan Institute for Arabic & Islamic Studies
London, 6th of April 2016

License to Transmit (*ijazah*)

All praise is due to Allah who connects whom He wills, with what He wills, to Him. The Erecter of proofs that guide unto Him. The Pre-eternal, Everlasting, the One, the All-Knowing. He is the Bestower of enabling-grace (*tawfiq*) to the straight path. May prayers and peace be upon the leader of the people of love and guidance, and his family, and his Companions. To proceed:

Truly, I connect to Shaykh al-Islam, Burhan al-Din, Ibrahim bin Muhammad al-Bajuri (may Allah have mercy upon him) from various routes of transmission, among the highest [shortest] of them is our narration on the authority of our Shaykh, the former Mufti of Egypt, Imam Ali Jumu'ah al-Shafi, on the authority of his Shaykh, the Sayyid, Abdullah b. al-Siddiq al-Ghumari al-Tanji (died 1410 AH), on the authority of the man who was granted a long life, Muhammad Duwaydar al-Kafrawi al-Talawi, on the authority of the Imam, Shaykh al-Islam, Burhan al-Din al-Bajuri (died at the end of 1277 AH). And via another chain also narrated by Shaykh Ali Jumu'ah, on the authority of the Sayyid, Muhammad Zaki al-Din Ibrahim al-Khalil, on the authority of Muhammad b. Abdullah al-Aquri al-Libi, on the authority of al-Bajuri. And in another chain, I also connect to Burhan al-Din al-Bajuri via the route of transmission of our Shaykh, the Sayyid, Abd al-Rahman b. Abd al-Hayy al-Kittani, on the authority of his father, the Sayyid, Abd al-Hayy, on the authority of al-Shihab Ahmad al-Rifa'i, on the authority of al-Bajuri.

I have licensed the brother for the sake of Allah Most High, *Rashad Jameer*, to transmit and translate the *Primer of Imam al-Bajuri on the Knowledge of Divine Unicity* (*'ilm al-Tawhid*) with a specific license. He has recited it to me and reviewed its points with me during my stay in Canada in the month of Ramadan of 1436 AH. I ask him to supplicate for me in private and in public.

Said by the tongue of and written by the pen of Shihab al-Din Ahmed b. Muhammad b. al-Sayyid Saad al-Azhari, al-Hasani in the city of our master, the Messenger of Allah ﷺ in Rabi al-Anwar 1437 AH – December 2015.

SHAYKH AHMAD SAAD AL-AZHARI

بسـم الله الرحمن الرحيم

الحمد لله واصل من شاء إليه بما شاء وناصب الدلائل الدالة عليه فهو القديم الباقي الواحد العليم، وهو المتفضل بالتوفيق إلى الصراط المستقيم والصلاة والسلام على إمام أهل الدلال والدلالة وآله وصحبه وبعد:

فإنني أتصل بشيخ الإسلام برهان الدين إبراهيم بن محمد الباجوري (رحمه الله تعالى) من طرق من أعلاها روايتنا عن شيخنا مفتي الديار المصرية السابق الإمام/ علي جمعة الشافعي عن شيخه السيد/ عبد الله بن الصديق الغماري الطنجي (ت: ١٤١٠ هـ) عن المعمر/ محمد دويدار الكفراوي التلاوي عن الإمام شيخ الإسلام/ برهان الدين الباجوري (توفي في حدود ١٢٦٧ هـ)

(ح) ويروي الشيخ علي جمعة أيضا عن السيد/ محمد زكي الدين إبراهيم الخليلي عن/ محمد بن عبد الله العاقوري الليبي عن الإمام الباجوري.

(ح) وأتصل أيضا بالبرهان الباجوري من طريق شيخنا السيد/ عبد الرحمن بن عبد الحي الكتاني عن والده السيد/ عبد الحي عن/ الشهاب أحمد الرفاعي عن/ الباجوري.

وقد أجزت الأخ في الله تعالى/ رشاد جمير برواية وترجمة رسالة الإمام الباجوري في علم التوحيد إجازة خاصة وقد قرأها عليَّ وحرّر بعض مسائلها أثناء إقامتي بكندا في شهر رمضان ١٤٣٦ هـ وأسأله صالح الدعوات في الخلوات والجلوات.

قاله بلسانه وكتبه ببنانه
شهاب الدين أحمد بن السيد محمد سعد الأزهري الحسني
في مدينة سيدنا رسول الله ربيع الأنور ١٤٣٧ هـ – ديسمبر ٢٠١٥

V

Publisher's Message

Very little debate and thought went into the decision on which of the intended topics of the IGI Essentials Book Series should be published first. Because, without a doubt, the times we live in have seen a wave of atheism and agnosticism spread far and wide around the world – including that of the Muslim majority nations.

As a child, many are taught something that more or less resembles the following: The Qur'an is a divine text revealed to the Prophet Muhammad ﷺ, who himself came as a mercy to mankind to teach us how to live. To live our life in accordance with the Qur'an and Sunna will ultimately mean entrance into Heaven. A young child accepts this and will typically not question the reality of these statements above. However, time and time again, I have personally witnessed (and I trust you have too) that as many individuals have grown older, they begin to question and doubt their faith. In the context of this situation, the worst thing that can happen is to leave that doubt unresolved.

Unfortunately, there are a plethora of reasons we could discuss, yet many Muslims never resolve the doubts and insecurities they have about their faith. Left unchecked, this has, in many instances, caused people to either leave the faith or become agnostic. A few years ago, our beloved teacher, Shaykh Hamza Yusuf, mentioned that for the first time since converting to Islam nearly 40 years ago, he is receiving pleas from concerned parents whose children have openly left Islam. The concern regarding Muslim youth who no longer identify with our faith is something I deeply worry about.

That being said, we ventured to publish this wonderful work by the Esteemed Imam of Masjid al-Azhar, Imam al-Bajuri, knowing that the need to study 'aqidah has never been stronger. The word 'aqidah comes from the Arabic root of 'aqada which means to hold tightly and make a knot. This is the way every Muslim should feel when it comes to the fundamental beliefs of Islam. We should all have a firm belief and strong conviction. It is our hope and aspiration that this text will serve to introduce, enhance, and solidify the belief of Muslims all over the English-speaking world. Keeping the primary aim and objective of the student of sacred knowledge in mind, this text comes with an allocated space for personal notes whilst studying the text. May Allah bless the author, the translator, and the members of our team at the Imam Ghazali Institute.

I close by asking that should you, the student, benefit from this text, please remember this needy servant and his family in your duas.

MUHAMMAD ADNAAN SATTAUR
Executive Director, Imam Ghazali Institute
May 10th, 2017 – Cairo, Egypt

Translator's Preface

In the name of Allah, most Gracious, most Merciful, the only Entity free of need, worthy of all praise. May peace and blessings be upon our master Muhammad, the unlettered Prophet for the end of time, and upon his Family, his Companions, and all those who follow his way until Judgment Day.

Islamic theology or 'aqidah is one of the most important and central-most sciences of Islamic scholarship, as it expounds upon the creed of the Muslims. It allows one to learn the attributes of the Creator, the Prophets ﷺ, the unseen realm, and all matters pertaining to them. The study of this science allows one to remove any doubt and gain certitude in belief; it safeguards one from distorted and deviant ideas. It is for this reason that it is considered an individual obligation (*fard 'ayn*) upon every believing male and female to study and acquire this knowledge. It is no wonder that the founder of one of the four Sunni Schools of Law, Abu Hanifa, who was given the honorific title *'Imam al-A'zam'* or *'the greatest Imam,'* has entitled his book on creed *'al-Fiqh al-akbar'* or *'the greatest science to be understood.'*

﴿فَاعْلَمْ أَنَّهُ لَا إِلَهَ إِلَّا اللّٰهَ﴾

Allah states in the Qur'an: *Know that there is no god but Allah...* (Muhammad 47:19). This is but one of the proofs from which scholars derive that it is obligatory to know, with certainty, that there cannot be another god besides Allah. Imam al-Ghazali says: *'Your worship is not acceptable unless you know whom you are worshipping,'* and the Malikite jurist al-Akhdari states: *'The first obligation upon every legally responsible person is to rectify his creed.'*

﴿فَاسْأَلُوا أَهْلَ الذِّكْرِ إِنْ كُنْتُمْ لَا تَعْلَمُونَ﴾

The Qur'an instructs to: *Ask the people of Remembrance if you know not* (Nahl 16:43). While it is necessary, and not only recommended, in matters of law (*fiqh*) for one to follow a scholar who is supremely qualified to derive rulings directly from the Qur'an and Sunna, which in Arabic is called a mujtahid, it is not required for the average Muslim to know the proofs for prayer, fasting, and fiqh on the whole. When the Companions used to seek fatwa (religious edicts) from the learned among them, they did not ask them for the proofs.

Today, many Muslims have a misunderstanding that they need to know the evidences for how to pray and fast, etc. So, do Muslims have to learn evidences as to why they believe in Allah Most High? Regarding 'aqidah, scholars say they do.

In the following verse of the Qur'an, Almighty Allah blamed the disbelieving Quraysh for following their forefathers in belief without knowing the proofs (*taqlid fi al-'aqa'id*):

﴿وَإِذَا قِيلَ لَهُمْ تَعَالَوْا إِلَى مَا أَنْزَلَ اللَّهُ وَإِلَى الرَّسُولِ قَالُوا حَسْبُنَا مَا وَجَدْنَا عَلَيْهِ آبَاءَنَا أَوَلَوْ كَانَ آبَاؤُهُمْ لَا يَعْلَمُونَ شَيْئًا وَلَا يَهْتَدُونَ﴾

And when it is said to them: 'Come to what Allah hath revealed; come to the Apostle' they say: 'Enough for us are the ways we found our fathers following.' What!

Even though their fathers were void of knowledge and guidance? (Ma'ida 5:104)

Unfortunately, this sentiment is still echoed today when Muslims are asked, especially in the University environment, why they are Muslims. They think something along the lines of: 'I'm Muslim because my parents are Muslim' – and Allah's aid is sought!

Imam Abu al-Mansur al-Maturidi, the great Imam of Ahl al-Sunna wa al-Jama'ah (may Allah have mercy on him) and the founder of one of the two schools of creed, states: 'The muqallid in creed ('aqidah) is a disobedient believer (mu'min 'asi'). In other words, he is not a disbeliever, but is considered sinful. Why, you may ask? Because Allah has commanded in His final revelation that we must *Know that there is no god but Allah.* You will notice that most of what lies in Imam al-Bajuri's main text (*matn*) does not reference revelation (the Qur'an) and is based on logic and reason.

This is especially important for Muslims living in non-Muslim majority lands where, when asked 'why' they believe in God, saying 'because the Qur'an says so' is circular reasoning and insufficient (though it may suffice the believer). Thus, to compliment the logical focus of this topic, I have added corroborative proofs and references from the Qur'an and Sunna in the footnotes to further strengthen the points therein.

Ultimately, as a response to a request, Imam al-Bajuri outlines the core beliefs of the orthodox Sunni doctrine ('aqidah) that must be known by every Muslim. Designed to be studied with a teacher or read on one's own, this text will equip the student with sufficient knowledge of the essentials of Muslim theology to be able to distinguish truth from falsehood, orthodox from heterodox, Ahl al-Sunna wa al-Jama'a or Sunni Islam from other than it. It is hoped that by including the facing, vocalized Arabic script that 1) students of Sacred Knowledge will be aided in learning the language of the Qur'an, the Prophet ﷺ, and the 'ulama, 2) it will serve as a teaching aid for the 'ulama when teaching this text to reference the original work and 3) to preserve the actual words of Imam al-Bajuri. Anything indecorous in this rendering is from my nafs and my ignorance, and anything herein which is of benefit is from Allah, the blessing of the author, and the scholars who transmitted it.

RASHAD JAMEER
Wasila Press
3 May 2016–25 Rajab 1437 AH

Imam Ibrahim al-Bajuri al-Azhari

All praise belongs to Allah, the Lord of the worlds. May prayers and peace be upon our Master Muhammad, his Family and his Companions, entirely. He is Ibrahim b. Muhammad b. Ahmad al-Bajuri or al-Bayjuri—which is an ascription to a village within a few hours of Cairo named al-Bajur—the Shaykh of Islam and the Imam of Masjid al-Azhar. He was born 1198 AH / 1784 CE and lived in Giza during the French occupation when Napoleon entered Cairo. In the year 1213 AH / 1799 CE, he returned to Cairo and began studying in Masjid al-Azhar and gained popularity due to his immense knowledge.

He began teaching in al-Azhar in *Sha'ban* of 1216 *hijri* / 1801 CE and continued teaching until he passed away in *Dhu al-Hijja* of 1277 AH / 1861 CE. The majority of his written works are commentaries, footnotes, or marginalia (*hawashi*) on texts which were widespread during his era, the most important of them being:

BOOKS OF JURISPRUDENCE (FIQH)

1. Marginalia on the commentary of the text of *Ibn Abi Shuja'a* by Ibn al-Qasim

2. Marginalia on the commentary of the *al-Arjuzah al-Rahbiyyah* by al-Shanshuri

BOOKS ON THEOLOGY ('AQIDAH)

1. Marginalia on the commentary of al-Sanusi's *Umm al-Barahin*

2. Marginalia on the commentary of the Ibrahim al-Laqqani's *Jawharat al-Tawhid*

3. The commentary on the book of his teacher, Shaykh al-Fadili, entitled *Kifayat al-'Ulum fi ma yajibu alayhim min 'ilm al-Kalam*

BOOKS ON THE PROPHETIC BIOGRAPHY (SIRAH)

1. Marginalia on Shamail al-Tirmidhi

2. Marginalia on the Prophetic Nativity (*Mawlid*) compiled by Ibn Hajar al-Asqalani

3. Marginalia on the grammarian Ibn Hisham's explanation of the ode entitled *Banat Su'ad*

4. Marginalia on Khalid al-Azhari's commentary on al-Busiri's *Burda*

BOOKS ON GRAMMAR, LOGIC, AND RHETORIC

1. Marginalia on al-'Imriti's commentary on *Sanhaji's Ajrumiyyah*

2. Marginalia on al-Samarqandi's epistle on rhetoric

3. Marginalia on al-Sanusi's abridgment on logic

4. Marginalia on al-Akhdari's commentary on logic entitled *al-Sullam*

And this text in your hands, which is a simple yet compre-
hensive epistle on the most important foundations of Islamic
creed, the creed of the People of the Prophetic way and the
Majority of scholars, according to the creedal school (*madhab*)
of Imam Abu al-Hasan al-Ashari ⬥.

The Ten Principles

Muqaddimat al-'Ilm

إن مبادِي كلَّ فنٍّ عشرةٌ

الحدُّ والموضوعُ ثم الثمرةْ

ونسبةٌ وفضلُهُ والواضعْ

والاسمُ الاستمدادُ حكمُ الشارعْ

مسائل والبعضُ بالبعضِ اكتفى

ومن درى الجميعَ حازَ الشرفا

The preceding poem was gleaned from pages 39–40 of Imam al-Bajuri's famous commentary on *Jawharat al-Tawhid*, specifically the edition edited and annotated by the former Mufti of Egypt, Ali Jumu'ah. It encapsulates the ten foundational principles of every Islamic science. Traditionally, a teacher would begin by detailing '*The Ten Principles*' of the subject matter at hand. This gives the student an overview and introduction to the topic. Every Islamic science is known to have its own specific foundational principles.

1. The definition (*al-hadd*) knowledge that provides the ability to establish religious beliefs through proofs with certitude. It refers to singling out the object of worship (Allah) with worship (*'ibadah*) and correct beliefs (*'aqa'id*), and confirming His Essence, His Attributes, and His Acts.

2. The topic (*al-mawdu'*) the Essence of Allah Most High, which expounds upon what is necessary for Him, what is impossible for Him, and what is possible, and the same for the Messengers. And what is possible to lead one to the existence and presence of his Maker ﷻ and to super-rational matters (*sam'iyat*) in order to believe in them.

3. The fruit (*al-thamara*) the gnosis or true knowledge (*ma'rifa*) of Allah by definitive proofs as well as winning eternal felicity [in Paradise].

4. The merit (*fadluhu*) it is the noblest of sacred sciences by virtue of its ascription to the Essence of Allah Most High, the essence of His Messengers, and what relates to that.

5. The ascription (*nisbah*) it is indeed the foundational religious science, everything besides it is secondary. And it was well said by the one who proclaimed:

O you who seeks to be nourished by knowledge
Every knowledge is a servant to Islamic theology
You seek knowledge of jurisprudence to know rulings
Yet are heedless of the One who revealed the rulings

6. The founder (*al-wadi'*) Abu al-Hasan al-Ash'ari and those who follow him, and Abu al-Mansur al-Maturidi and those who follow him, meaning they codi-

fied Islamic theology in their books and refuted the obfuscations and heterodoxies of the Mu'tazilites.[1] Otherwise, Islamic monotheism was brought by every prophet since the time of Adam 🕊 until the Day of Judgment.

7. Its name (*al-ism*) al-Tawhid or monotheism because the research about Allah's Oneness (*wahdaniyyah*) is its most famous subject. It is also called: 'ilm al-kalam (literally knowledge that involves much discussion) because the former scholars used to say in their research on this subject *'there is much discussion about this...'* or because there was so much difference of opinion on issues of theology. And some scholars mention there are eight names for this subject.

8. The sources (*al-istimdad*) from both rational and transmitted textual proofs.

9. The ruling of the Lawgiver (*hukm al-shariʿ*) it is an individual obligation (*fard ʿayn*) upon every accountable soul, man or woman.

10. Issues covered (*masa'il*) examining what is necessary, possible, and impossible in connection with Allah and His Messengers 🕊.

---

1   Within the two Sunni Orthodox Schools of Creed (*ʿaqidah*), the Ash'ari and the Maturidi Schools, there are only semantic differences. One example of the minor verbal differences is that Ash'aris believe that man is responsible to believe in God because of revelation, not merely because he is endowed with human reason, and that he has no responsibility prior to revelation, while Maturidis believe that man is responsible to believe in God even before revelation, by the mere fact of having reason. (See Shaykh Nuh Keller, The Ashari and the Maturidi Schools)

رسالة في علم التوحيد

INTRODUCTION TO ISLAMIC CREED
Risālat fi 'Ilm al-Tawhīd

Compiled by
Imam Ibrahim al-Bajuri

Translation & Notes by
Rashad Jameer

In the name of Allah, the Beneficent, the Merciful.
Praise be to Allah,[2] Lord of the worlds. May prayers
and peace be showered upon the Messenger of
Allah ﷺ

Says the remiss one in need of the mercy of his Omniscient
and All-Seeing Lord, Ibrahim al-Bajuri, informs that a brother,
may Allah reform him and me, asked me to write for him a
good treatise dealing with the attributes of the Lord and their
antitheses,[3] what is permissible for Him Most High, what are
the attributes that are rationally necessary for the divine messengers (*al-rusul*), what attributes are rationally possible for
them, and what attributes are rationally impossible for them.
So, I undertook this effort to comply with his request. All en-
abling grace belongs to Allah, so seeking His aid I declare:

---

2   There are three possible meanings for the 'Alif Lam' in the
beginning of 'Al-hamdulilah'. 1) All types of praise (*jince*) belongs
to Allah 2) Allah's praise of Himself in pre-eternity ('*ahd*) or 3) an
all-encompassing praise that belongs to Allah (*istighraq*). (Sa'd al-Din
al-Taftazani, Sharh al-'Aqidah al-Nasafiyyah)
3   Their opposites.

اَلْحَمْدُ للهِ رَبِّ الْعَالَمِيْنَ، وَالصَّلَاةُ وَالسَّلَامُ عَلَىٰ رَسُوْلِ اللهِ صَلَّى اللهُ عَلَيْهِ وَسَلَّمَ.

وَبَعْدُ: فَيَقُوْلُ فَقِيْرُ رَحْمَةِ رَبِّهِ الْخَبِيْرِ الْبَصِيْرِ، إِبْرَاهِيْم الْبَاجُوْرِيُّ ذُو التَّقْصِيْرِ: طَلَبَ مِنِّيْ بَعْضُ الْإِخْوَانِ - أَصْلَحَ اللهُ لِيْ وَلَهُمُ الْحَالَ وَالشَّأْنَ - أَنْ أَكْتُبَ لَهُ رِسَالَةً لَطِيْفَةً، تَشْتَمِلُ عَلَىٰ صِفَاتِ الْمَوْلَىٰ وَأَضْدَادِهَا، وَمَا يَجُوْزُ فِيْ حَقِّهِ تَعَالَىٰ، وَعَلَىٰ مَا يَجِبُ فِيْ حَقِّ الرُّسُلِ وَمَا يَسْتَحِيْلُ فِيْ حَقِّهِمْ وَمَا يَجُوْزُ،

Every accountable soul [that is, every sane soul possessed of reason by having come of age through the attainment of puberty] is obliged [by sacred law (*al-shari'ah*)] to know what is rationally necessary for Him Most High, what is possible for Him, and what is impossible for Him.

يَجِبُ عَلَى كُلِّ مُكَلَّفٍ أَنْ يَعْرِفَ مَا يَجِبُ فِيْ حَقِّهِ تَعَالَى، وَ مَا يَسْتَحِيْلُ، وَ مَا يَجُوْزُ

Allah's Attributes ﷻ

Existence[4] (*Wujud*) is necessary for Him ﷻ. The proof for
that is the existence of creation.[5] Its opposite is **non-existence**
(*'adam*).

---

4   This sole attribute, wujud (Existence) is classified in theology as
Sifah nafsiyyah referring to the attribute of Allah's Essence (*dhat*).
Another related point is Allah being '*wajib al-wujud*' or 'the only
necessary existence,' whereas everyone and everything else is contin-
gent. In other words, everything depends on Him and He depends
on none. The Qur'an declares in Surah al-Ikhlas, in verses 1–2, *Say*
(O Muhammad): "*He is Allah, the Unique. Allah the Independent*"
(Allah al-Samad).

$$﴿ قُلْ هُوَ اللَّهُ أَحَدٌ اللَّهُ الصَّمَدُ ﴾$$

(al-Ikhlas 112:1–2)

Scholars of Qur'an and Arabic language say 'Samad' refers to the
being who needs none, but all are in need of Him.
5   Creation logically requires an originator. The rational proof for
that is as follows: 1) The world and everything in it is constant-
ly undergoing countless forms of change. 2) Every change of state
necessarily implies the origination of a new state. 3) Therefore, the
world and all that is in it is originated and has an originator, otherwise known as Allah.

الصِّفَة النَّفْسِيَّة

فَيَجِبُ فِي حَقِّهِ تَعَالَى: [اَلْوُجُوْدُ] - وَ ضِدُّهُ [الْعَدَمُ]، وَ الدَّلِيْلُ عَلَى ذلِكَ: وُجُوْدُ الْمَخْلُوْقَاتِ

Beginninglessness [6] (*Qidam*) is necessary for Him ﷻ. It means that He ﷻ has no beginning. The proof for that is: were He to be originated, He would have needed an originator, which is impossible.[7] Its opposite is **origination** (contingency) (*al-huduth*) [which is the characteristic of every contingent thing or quality which comes into existence after having not existed.]

---

6   This word can also carry the meanings of pre-eternal, eternal, or ancientness. The Qur'an states in Surah Hadid, verse 3, *He is the First, the Last, the Manifest, the Hidden....* The traits of Beginninglessness, Endlessness, Difference from originated beings, Self-Subsistence and Oneness are categorized as Sifah salbiyyah (negating attributes) because they negate what does not befit Allah.

$$\text{هُوَ الْأَوَّلُ وَالْآخِرُ وَالظَّاهِرُ وَالْبَاطِنُ ۝ وَهُوَ بِكُلِّ شَيْءٍ عَلِيمٌ}$$

(Hadid 57:3)

7   Since His existence ﷻ is rationally necessary, not merely possible or contingent, as was indicated in the note of the first attribute called wajib al-wujud or the only necessary existence.

الصِّفَات السَّلبِيَّة

وَ يَجِبُ فِي حَقِّهِ تَعَالَى: [اَلْقِدَمُ] - وَ مَعْنَاهُ أَنَّهُ لَا أَوَّلَ لَهُ تَعَالَى وَضِدُّهُ [الْحُدُوْثُ]، وَ الدَّلِيْلُ عَلَى ذلِكَ: أَنَّهُ لَوْ كَانَ حَادِثًا لَاحْتَاجَ إِلَى مُحْدِثٍ وَ هُوَ مُحَالٌ. وَ يَجِبُ فِي حَقِّهِ تَعَالَى:

Endlessness[8] (*al-Baqa'*) is indeed necessary for Him ﷻ, which means that nothing comes after Him, exalted is He. The proof for endlessness is were He to be transient, He would have been contingent, which is impossible. Its opposite is transience[9] (*al-fana'*).

---

8   The Qur'an states, *What is with you perishes, while that which is with Allah Lasts* (Nahl 16:96) and *Everyone on it shall perish, while the Face of your Lord abides, the Possessor of Majesty and Generosity* (Rahman 55:26–27).

مَا عِندَكُمْ يَنفَدُ ۟ وَمَا عِندَ اللَّهِ بَاقٍ ۟ وَلَنَجْزِيَنَّ
الَّذِينَ صَبَرُوا أَجْرَهُم بِأَحْسَنِ مَا كَانُوا يَعْمَلُونَ

(Nahl 16:96)

كُلُّ مَنْ عَلَيْهَا فَانٍ ۟ وَيَبْقَىٰ وَجْهُ رَبِّكَ ذُو الْجَلَالِ
وَالْإِكْرَامِ

(Rahman 55:26–27)

9   That is, extinction.

[اَلْبَقَاءُ] - وَ مَعْنَاهُ أَنَّهُ تَعَالَى لَا آخِرَ لَهُ - وَ ضِدُّهُ

[الْفَنَاءُ]، وَ الدَّلِيلُ عَلَى ذلِكَ: أَنَّهُ لَوْ كَانَ فَانِيًا

لَكَانَ حَادِثًا وَ هُوَ مُحَالٌ

Dissimilarity to originated beings[10] (al-Mukhalafah lil-hawa-dith) is necessary for Him ﷻ. It means that He ﷻ is not like originated things. Thus, He has no hand, no eye, no ear, nor anything else from the attributes of originated things.[11]

The proof for that is: were He to resemble originated things, He would have been originated, which is impossible. Its opposite is resemblance (al-mumathalah).[12]

---

10   The Qur'an states, *There is nothing like His likeness...* (Shura' 42:11) and *there is none similar to He* (Ikhlas 112:4). Furthermore, Allah is not in need of time and space; on the contrary, time and space are in need of Him ﷻ. Also, the following supportive statement is attributed to Abu Bakr al-Siddique ؓ, 'Everything your mind can conceive, Allah is utterly dissimilar indeed!' (*kulla ma khatara bi balik, Allahu khilafu dhalik*).

لَيْسَ كَمِثْلِهِ شَىْءٌ ۖ وَهُوَ السَّمِيعُ الْبَصِيرُ

(Shura' 42:11)

وَلَمْ يَكُن لَّهُ كُفُوًا أَحَدٌ

(Ikhlas 112:4)

11   To understand verses that, on the surface, state Allah has a created attribute like a hand, eye etc., scholars say one should apply conclusive verses (muhkam ayats) to the ambiguous verses. Meaning, when we read verses like *the Hand of Allah is over their hands...* or *...surely you are before Our eyes...* which are ambiguous verses, one should compare them to conclusive (*muhkam*) verses such as *And there is none like unto Him...* and *there is nothing whatever like unto Him....* These conclusive verses remove the possibility of Allah having anything similar to Him; therefore, since we have physical body parts, it follows that Allah Most High cannot. Thereafter, whatever Allah intended by those ambiguous verses we firmly believe in and resign their meanings to Allah, termed in Arabic as *tafwid*. This was the way of the Pious Forbears (salaf al-salihin).

12   Note: many people who become exposed to the topic of assigning a meaning to ambiguous verses (ta'wil) can initially become obsessed about the polemics surrounding this topic when hearing these verses,

وَ يَجِبُ فِي حَقِّهِ تَعَالَى: [اَلْمُخَالَفَةُ لِلْحَوَادِثِ]
- وَ مَعْنَاهُ أَنَّهُ تَعَالَى لَيْسَ مُمَاثِلًا لِلْحَوَادِثِ،
فَلَيْسَ لَهُ يَدٌ وَ لاَ عَيْنٌ وَ لاَ أُذُنٌ وَ لاَ غَيْرُ ذلِكَ
مِنْ صِفَاتِ الْحَوَادِثِ - وَ ضِدُّهَا [الْمُمَاثَلَةُ]، وَ
الدَّلِيْلُ عَلَى ذلِكَ: أَنَّهُ لَوْ كَانَ مُمَاثِلًا لِلْحَوَادِثِ
لَكَانَ حَادِثًا وَ هُوَ مُحَالٌ

---

and can actually forget Allah's providence, and the sentiment and emotion contained in the actual verse. An example of restoring the subtlety back to such verses was given when discussing the verse *the All-Merciful assumed the Throne* (al-Rahman 'ala al-'Arsh ista-wa) that normally when someone assumes leadership or authority in this world, they do so with a sense of power, might, and majesty. But notice when Allah mentions assuming the Throne, He didn't mention his name, Jabbar (Compeller), or 'Aziz (Almighty) or Jalil (The Majestic), which would have been appropriate and expected. Instead, He mentioned in the verse to highlight His dominant trait of mercy, His holy name al-Rahman (All-Merciful) to remind us, even in His supreme authority, 'My mercy supersedes My wrath.'

Self-Subsistence[13] (*al-Qiyamu bi al-nafs*) is necessary for Him ﷻ. It means He ﷻ does not need a locus [to exist] or determinant. The proof for that is that were He to require a locus [to subsist], He would have been an attribute, and His being an attribute is impossible; and were He to require a determinant, He would have been originated, and His being originated is impossible. Its opposite is **requiring a locus [to exist] or determinant**[14] (*al-ihtiyaj ila al-mahall wa al-mukhassas*).

---

13   The Qur'an states, *Allah; there is no God but He; the Ever-Living, the Self-Subsisting…* (Baqara 2:255)

اللَّهُ لَا إِلَهَ إِلَّا هُوَ الْحَيُّ الْقَيُّومُ ۞ لَا تَأْخُذُهُ سِنَةٌ وَلَا نَوْمٌ ۞ لَهُ مَا فِي السَّمَاوَاتِ وَمَا فِي الْأَرْضِ ۞ مَن ذَا الَّذِى يَشْفَعُ عِندَهُ إِلَّا بِإِذْنِهِ ۞ يَعْلَمُ مَا بَيْنَ أَيْدِيهِمْ وَمَا خَلْفَهُمْ ۞ وَلَا يُحِيطُونَ بِشَىْءٍ مِّنْ عِلْمِهِ إِلَّا بِمَا شَاءَ ۞ وَسِعَ كُرْسِيُّهُ السَّمَاوَاتِ وَالْأَرْضَ ۞ وَلَا يَئُودُهُ حِفْظُهُمَا ۞ وَهُوَ الْعَلِىُّ الْعَظِيمُ

(Baqara 2:255)

14   According to Shaykh Abdul Aziz Suraqah, "the proof that Allah is absolutely Self-Subsistent—meaning, Independent and not an attribute of something else or subsisting in something else—is that if He subsisted in something else, He would be a quality of that thing. But qualities cannot be described by other qualities, so if Allah was a quality of something else it would be impossible to describe Him as All-Seeing, All-Hearing, Powerful, etc. Let us use the example of a red car. Red is the quality of the car. It describes it. The color white is also a quality; but it is impossible for red to be a quality of white, or vice versa, because neither color has an independent existence. It is absurd to say, "This red is white and this white is red."

Similarly, to say that Allah subsists in something else implies that He is a quality of that thing and in need of it in order to subsist. That would mean that He is a possible existent. This, as we have learned, is rationally impossible. If we consider the belief of most Christians we will see that they violate this tenet of belief. They believe in di-

16

وَ يَجِبُ فِي حَقِّهِ تَعَالَى: [اَلْقِيَامُ بِالنَّفْسِ] - وَ مَعْنَاهُ أَنَّهُ تَعَالَى
لَا يَفْتَقِرُ إِلَى مَحَلٍّ، وَ لَا إِلَى مُخَصِّصٍ - وَ ضِدُّهُ [اَلْاِحْتِيَاجُ
إِلَى الْمَحَلِّ وَ الْمُخَصِّصِ]، وَ الدَّلِيلُ عَلَى ذَلِكَ: أَنَّهُ لَو احْتَاجَ
إِلَى مَحَلٍّ لَكَانَ صِفَةً، وَ كَوْنُهُ صِفَةً مُحَالٌ، وَ لَو احْتَاجَ إِلَى
مُخَصِّصٍ لَكَانَ حَادِثًا وَ كَوْنُهُ حَادِثًا مُحَالٌ

vine incarnation and say that Allah dwells within the body of Jesus
Christ ﷺ. This belief is false and implies that Allah is a quality of
Prophet Jesus ﷺ. It also implies that Allah is divisible into parts,
which, as we will see, is also rationally impossible. If Allah required
a determiner He would be contingent, and if He was contingent He
would not be pre-eternal, which, as we have learned, is rationally
impossible. Allah is absolutely independent and dissimilar to His
creation. Everything created by Allah has a beginning, a particular
shape or size, and undergoes change. All created forms and attributes, such as shapes and qualities, have a beginning and an end,
so it is impossible that Allah should resemble them in any way. If
Allah resembled creation He would also be subject to change, and,
as explained earlier, anything that is subject to change is a possible
existent and cannot be divine. It is rationally impossible for Allah to
have any attribute that is possible—all of His attributes are necessary.
If something resembles another thing in creation (like how a cat's
paw resembles a dog's paw, or how a coffee table resembles a dinner
table), it means that it will have limits and boundaries that must
be created. Since they are merely possible they must have a creator
to specify their limits. If you pointed to a phone and asked, "Who
made this phone in this particular shape?" and someone answered,
"No one made it; it is like that eternally," you would call the answer
absurd. Anything with limits needs someone or something to specify it. Islamic theologians mention an important principle in this
regard: "Anything described with contingent qualities must also be
contingent." If we say that an object has a particular size, no smaller
or larger, it is rationally possible for us to say that it can be larger or
smaller than it is. Since that is possible, it can be asked, "Why isn't
the object larger or smaller than it is?" And if the object accepts
multiple possibilities, it must be contingent; otherwise it would be
a case of infinite regress."

17

Oneness[15] (al-Wahdaniyyah) is necessary for Him ﷻ in entity, in attributes, and in acts. The meaning of oneness in entity is that He is not composed of parts. The meaning of oneness in attributes is that He does not have two or more attributes of one kind, such as two 'powers', and none other than He has any attributes resembling His attribute ﷻ.

The meaning of oneness in acts is that none other than Allah ﷻ has any act [like His]. The proof for that is if He were more than one, none of these created things would have existed.[16] Its opposite is **multiplicity** (al-ta'addud).

---

15   The Qur'an states, *Your God is One God* (Nahl 16:22) and *And our God and your God is one; and we are Muslims (in submission) to Him* (Ankabut 29:46)

إِلَٰهُكُمْ إِلَٰهٌ وَاحِدٌ ۚ فَالَّذِينَ لَا يُؤْمِنُونَ بِالْآخِرَةِ
قُلُوبُهُم مُّنكِرَةٌ وَهُم مُّسْتَكْبِرُونَ

(Nahl 16:22)

وَلَا تُجَادِلُوا أَهْلَ الْكِتَابِ إِلَّا بِالَّتِي هِيَ أَحْسَنُ إِلَّا الَّذِينَ
ظَلَمُوا مِنْهُمْ ۖ وَقُولُوا آمَنَّا بِالَّذِي أُنزِلَ إِلَيْنَا وَأُنزِلَ
إِلَيْكُمْ وَإِلَٰهُنَا وَإِلَٰهُكُمْ وَاحِدٌ وَنَحْنُ لَهُ مُسْلِمُونَ

(Ankabut 29:46)

16   The Qur'an states, *if there were in the heavens and the earth, other gods besides Allah, there would be confusion in both [the Heavens and earth]! But glory be to Allah, the Lord of the Throne: High is He above what they attribute to Him!* (Anbiya' 21:22)

لَوْ كَانَ فِيهِمَا آلِهَةٌ إِلَّا اللَّهُ لَفَسَدَتَا ۚ فَسُبْحَانَ اللَّهِ رَبِّ
الْعَرْشِ عَمَّا يَصِفُونَ

(Anbiya' 21:22)

وَ يَجِبُ فِي حَقِّهِ تَعَالَى: [اَلْوَحْدَانِيَّةُ] فِي الذَّاتِ وَ فِي الصِّفَاتِ وَ فِي الْأَفْعَالِ. وَ مَعْنَى الْوَحْدَانِيَّةِ فِي الذَّاتِ: أَنَّهَا لَيْسَتْ مُرَكَّبَةً مِنْ أَجْزَاءٍ مُتَعَدِّدَة

وَ مَعْنَى الْوَحْدَانِيَّة فِي الصِّفَاتِ: أَنَّهُ لَيْسَ لَهُ صِفَتَانِ فَأَكْثَر مِنْ جِنْسٍ وَاحِدٍ كَقُدْرَتَيْنِ, وَ هَكَذَا, وَ لَيْسَ لِغَيْرِهِ صِفَةٌ تُشَابِهُ صِفَتَهُ تَعَالَى

وَ مَعْنَى الْوَحْدَانِيَّةِ فِي الْأَفْعَالِ: أَنَّهُ لَيْسَ لِغَيْرِهِ فِعْلٌ مِنَ الْأَفْعَالِ. وَ ضِدُّهَا [اَلتَّعَدُّدُ]، وَ الدَّلِيلُ عَلَى ذَلِكَ: أَنَّهُ لَوْ كَانَ مُتَعَدِّدًا لَمْ يُوجَدْ شَيْءٌ مِن هَذِهِ الْمَخْلُوقَات

Power[17] (*al-Qudrah*) is necessary for Him ﷻ. It is a pre-eternal attribute subsisting through His Entity ﷻ with which He brings things into existence and takes them out of existence. The proof for that is that were He unable, nothing of the creation would have existed.[18] Its opposite is **inability** (*al-'ajz*).

---

17   The Qur'an states, *Indeed, Allah has Power over all things* (Baqara 2:20). The traits of Power, Will, Knowledge, Life, Hearing, and Seeing are classified as sifat al-ma'ani (qualitative attributes) and subsists with the Entity of Allah, and necessarily predicates that He ﷻ, not only has the particular quality (e.g. Knowledge), but is Knowledgeable, or in theological parlance, is being Knowledgeable, as will come in the following category of traits.

يَكَادُ الْبَرْقُ يَخْطَفُ أَبْصَارَهُمْ ۖ كُلَّمَا أَضَاءَ لَهُم مَّشَوْا فِيهِ وَإِذَا أَظْلَمَ عَلَيْهِمْ قَامُوا ۚ وَلَوْ شَاءَ اللَّهُ لَذَهَبَ بِسَمْعِهِمْ وَأَبْصَارِهِمْ ۚ إِنَّ اللَّهَ عَلَىٰ كُلِّ شَيْءٍ قَدِيرٌ

(Baqara 2:20)

18   This statement predicates that Allah's performance of a thing should not logically be impossible. Hence, the question many atheists pose 'Can God create a rock so heavy He cannot lift?', is a rational impossibility, an absurdity. This is similar to the case if someone were to ask you to make a square circle. It is a rational impossibility.

صِفَات المَعَني

وَ يَجِبُ فِي حَقِّهِ تَعَالَى: [اَلْقُدْرَةُ] - وَ هِيَ صِفَةٌ قَدِيْمَةٌ قَائِمَةٌ بِذَاتِهِ تَعَالَى يوجد بِهَا وَ يُعْدِمُ - وَ ضِدُّهَا [اَلْعَجْزُ]، وَ الدَّلِيْلُ عَلَى ذَلِكَ: أَنَّهُ لَوْ كَانَ عَاجِزًا لَمْ يُوْجَدْ شَيْءٌ مِنْ هَذِهِ الْمَخْلُوقَات

21

Will[19] (*al-Iradah*) is necessary for Him ﷻ. It is a pre-eternal attribute subsisting through His Entity ﷻ with which He determines possible existence or non-existence, independence or dependence, knowledge or ignorance, etc. The proof for that is, were He compelled, He would have been unable, and His being unable is impossible. Its opposite is **compulsion** (*al-karahah*).

---

19   The Qur'an states, [*God is the*] *Doer of what He wills* (Hud 11:107) and …*except what Allah wills* ('Ala 87:7) and *We raise the ranks of whomsoever We will…* (Yusuf 12:76)

خَالِدِينَ فِيهَا مَا دَامَتِ السَّمَاوَاتُ وَالْأَرْضُ إِلَّا مَا شَاءَ
رَبُّكَ ۚ إِنَّ رَبَّكَ فَعَّالٌ لِّمَا يُرِيدُ ۝

(Hud 11:107)

إِلَّا مَا شَاءَ اللَّهُ ۚ إِنَّهُ يَعْلَمُ الْجَهْرَ وَمَا يَخْفَىٰ ۝

('Ala 87:7)

…نَرْفَعُ دَرَجَاتٍ مَّن نَّشَاءُ ۗ وَفَوْقَ كُلِّ ذِى عِلْمٍ عَلِيمٌ ۝

(Yusuf 12:76)

22

وَ يَجِبُ فِي حَقِّهِ تَعَالَى: [اَلْإِرَادَةُ] - وَهِيَ صِفَةٌ قَدِيمَةٌ قَائِمَةٌ بِذَاتِهِ تَعَالَى يُخَصِّصُ بِهَا الْمُمْكِنَ بِالْوُجُودِ أَوْ بِالْعَدَمِ أَوْ بِالْغِنَى أَوْ بِالْفَقْرِ أَوْ بِالْعِلْمِ أَوْ بِالْجَهْلِ إِلَى غَيْرِ ذَلِكَ، وَضِدُّهَا [اَلْكَرَاهَةُ]، وَ الدَّلِيْلُ عَلَى ذَلِكَ: أَنَّهُ لَوْ كَانَ كَارِهًا لَكَانَ عَاجِزًا، وَكَوْنُهُ عَاجِزًا مُحَالٌ

23

Knowledge[20] (*al-'Ilm*) is necessary for Him ﷻ. It is a pre-eternal attribute subsisting through His entity ﷻ with which He knows [all] things.

The proof for that is were He ignorant, He would not have been willing, which is impossible. Its opposite is **ignorance** (*al-jahl*).

---

20   The Qur'an states, ...*and above every one possessed of knowledge is the All-Knowing* (Yusuf 12:76) and *Our Lord! Accept (this service) from us: for thou are the All-Hearing, the All-Knowing* (Baqara 2:127)

فَبَدَأَ بِأَوْعِيَتِهِمْ قَبْلَ وِعَاءِ أَخِيهِ ثُمَّ اسْتَخْرَجَهَا مِن وِعَاءِ

أَخِيهِ ۚ كَذَٰلِكَ كِدْنَا لِيُوسُفَ ۖ مَا كَانَ لِيَأْخُذَ أَخَاهُ فِي دِينِ

الْمَلِكِ إِلَّا أَن يَشَاءَ اللَّهُ ۚ نَرْفَعُ دَرَجَاتٍ مَّن نَّشَاءُ ۗ وَفَوْقَ كُلِّ

ذِى عِلْمٍ عَلِيمٌ ۝

(Yusuf 12:76)

وَإِذْ يَرْفَعُ إِبْرَاهِيمُ الْقَوَاعِدَ مِنَ الْبَيْتِ وَإِسْمَاعِيلُ رَبَّنَا

تَقَبَّلْ مِنَّا ۖ إِنَّكَ أَنتَ السَّمِيعُ الْعَلِيمُ ۝

(Baqara 2:127)

24

وَ يَجِبُ فِي حَقِّهِ تَعَالَى: [الْعِلْمُ] - وَهِيَ صِفَةٌ قَدِيمَةٌ قَائِمَةٌ بِذَاتِهِ تَعَالَى يَعْلَمُ بِهَا الْأَشْيَاء - وَضِدُّهَا [الْجَهْلُ]، وَ الدَّلِيلُ عَلَى ذَلِكَ: أَنَّهُ لَوْ كَانَ جَاهِلًا لَمْ يَكُنْ مُرِيدًا وَهُوَ مُحَالٌ

Life[21] (*al-Hayat*) is necessary for Him ﷻ. It is a pre-eternal attribute subsisting through His Entity ﷻ, which validates His being attributed with knowledge and the other attributes. The proof for that is, were He dead, He would not have been able, willing, or knowledgeable, which is impossible. Its opposite is death[22] (*al-mawt*).

---

21   The Qur'an states, …*the Ever-Living, the Subsisting* (Baqara 2:255)

اللَّهُ لَا إِلَهَ إِلَّا هُوَ الْحَيُّ الْقَيُّومُ ۚ ... ۞

(Baqara 2:255)

22   This is substantiated in a hadith, an excerpt of which follows, '…He is Living and never dies.' (Tirmidhi 2:181) And in another rigorously authenticated hadith narrated by the mother of the believers, 'A'isha ﵂, at the passing of the Prophet ﷺ that Abu Bakr ﵁ stood up amidst the confusion that ensued and said, 'No doubt! Whoever worshipped Muhammad, then Muhammad has passed, but whoever worshipped Allah, then Allah is Alive and shall never die.' (Bukhari, Book 5, Volume 57, Hadith 19)

وَ يَجِبُ فِي حَقِّهِ تَعَالَى: [اَلْحَيَاةُ] - وَهِيَ صِفَةٌ
قَدِيمَةٌ قَائِمَةٌ بِذَاتِهِ تَعَالَى تُصَحِّحُ لَهُ أَنْ يَتَّصِفَ
بِالْعِلْمِ وَغَيْرِهِ مِنَ الصِّفَاتِ - وَضِدُّهَا [اَلْمَوْتُ]
- وَ الدَّلِيْلُ عَلَى ذَلِكَ: أَنَّهُ لَوْ كَانَ مَيِّتًا لَمْ يَكُنْ
قَادِرًا وَلَا مُرِيْدًا وَلَا عَالِمًا وَهُوَ مُحَالٌ

Hearing and sight (*al-Sam' wa al-Basar*) are necessary for Him ﷻ. They are two pre-eternal attributes subsisting through His Entity through which existence is disclosed. The proof for that is His statement ﷻ, *And He is The All-Hearing, The All-Seeing* (*Shura'* 42:11). Their opposites are **deafness and blindness** (*al-sumum wa al-'ama*).

Speech (*al-Kalam*) is necessary for Him ﷻ. It is a pre-eternal attribute subsisting through His entity ﷻ that is not of letters or sounds. The proof for that is His statement ﷻ, *And Allah spoke to Musa directly* (*Nisa'* 4:164). Its opposite is **muteness** (*al-bukm*), **i.e. dumbness.**

وَ يَجِبُ فِي حَقِّهِ تَعَالَى: [اَلسَّمْعُ وَالْبَصَرُ] - وَهُمَا صِفَتَانِ قَدِيْمَتَانِ قَائِمَتَانِ بِذَاتِهِ تَعَالَى يَنْكَشِفُ بِهِمَا الْمَوْجُود - وَضِدُّهُمَا [الصَّمَمُ وَالْعَمَى]، وَ الدَّلِيْلُ عَلَى ذَلِكَ: قَوْلُهُ تَعَالَى: لَيْسَ كَمِثْلِهِ شَيْءٌ وَهُوَ السَّمِيعُ الْبَصِيرُ. [الشُّورَى]

وَ يَجِبُ فِي حَقِّهِ تَعَالَى: [اَلْكَلَامُ] - وَهُوَ صِفَةٌ قَدِيمَة قَائِمَةٌ بِذَاتِهِ تَعَالَى وَلَيْسَتْ بِحَرْفٍ وَلَا صَوْتٍ - وَضِدُّهَا [اَلْبُكْمُ] وَهُوَ الْخَرَسُ، وَ الدَّلِيْلُ عَلَى ذَلِكَ: قَوْلُهُ تَعَالَى: وَ كَلَّمَ اللهُ مُوسَى تَكْلِيمًا [اَلنِّسَاءُ]

His being All-Powerful (*kawnuhu Qadir*) is necessary for Him ﷻ. The proof for that is the proof of ability. Its opposite is His being unable (*kawnuhu 'ajiz*).[23]

His being Willing (*kawnuhu murid*) is necessary for Him ﷻ. The proof for that is the proof of will. Its opposite is His being compelled (*kawnuhu karih*).

---

23   This attribute (His being All-Powerful) and the following six attributes (His being Willing, All-Knowing, Living, Hearing, Seeing, and Speaking) are classified as *sifat al-ma'nawiyya* (predicative attributes) because they are ascribed to predicated meanings from the qualitative attributes. Allah being Powerful is necessarily implied by His attribute of Power, and similarly, His being Willing is necessarily implied by His attribute of Will, and so on for the remaining five attributes. The reason why these following seven predicative attributes (*sifat al-ma'nawiyya*) are necessary implications of the qualitative attributes (*sifat al-ma'ani*) is because all of the qualitative attributes are real attributes. Every real attribute, since it subsists within the one who is described with it, must acquire a state that cannot be affirmed without that attribute. So he who possesses power must acquire a state that he is powerful over that which his power is connected. This state is expressed by saying that he is All-Powerful with omnipotence. He who possesses knowledge must acquire a state, namely, that He is knowledgeable of that to which His Knowledge is linked. This state is expressed by saying that He is All-Knowing with omniscience, and the same is said for the remaining attributes. (Sanusi) This is an advanced aspect of theology, for more details see Sa'id Foudah's commentary on the Sanusi Creed.

الصِّفَات المَعَنويَّة

-وَ يَجِبُ فِي حَقِّهِ تَعَالَى: [كَوْنُهُ قَادِرًا] - وَضِدُّهُ [كَوْنُهُ عَاجِزًا]، وَ الدَّلِيْلُ عَلَى ذَلِكَ: دَلِيلُ الْقُدْرَة

وَ يَجِبُ فِي حَقِّهِ تَعَالَى: [كَوْنُهُ مريدًا] - وَضِدُّهُ [كَوْنُهُ كَارِهًا]، وَ الدَّلِيْلُ عَلَى ذَلِكَ: دَلِيْلُ الْإِرادة

His being All-Knowing (*kawnuhu 'alim*) is necessary for Him ﷻ. The proof for that is the proof of knowledge. Its opposite is His being ignorant (*kawnuhu jahil*).

His being Living (*kawnuhu hayy*) is necessary for Him ﷻ. The proof for that is the proof of life. Its opposite is His being dead (*kawnuhu mayyit*).

His being All-Hearing and All-Seeing (*kawnuhu sami' wa basir*) is necessary for Him ﷻ. The proof for that are the proof of hearing and the proof of sight. Their opposites are His being deaf and His being blind (*kawnuhu asamm wa kawnuhu a'ma*).

His being one who Speaks (*kawnuhu mutakallim*) is necessary for Him ﷻ. The proof for that is the proof of speech. Its opposite is His being mute (*kawnuhu abkam*).

THE POSSIBLE

Doing or leaving anything possible (*Fi'lu kulli mumkinin aw tarkuhu*) is possible for Him ﷻ. The proof is that if doing or leaving something was necessary upon Him ﷻ, the possible would become either necessary or impossible, which is impossible.

وَ يَجِبُ فِي حَقِّهِ تَعَالَى: [كَوْنُهُ عَالِمًا] - وَضِدُّهُ [كَوْنُهُ جَاهِلًا]، وَ الدَّلِيْلُ عَلَى ذَلِكَ: دَلِيْلُ العلم

وَ يَجِبُ فِي حَقِّهِ تَعَالَى: [كَوْنُهُ حَيًّا] - وَضِدُّهُ [كَوْنُهُ مَيِّتًا]، وَ الدَّلِيْلُ عَلَى ذلِكَ: دَلِيْلُ الْحَيَاة

وَ يَجِبُ فِي حَقِّهِ تَعَالَى: [كَوْنُهُ سَمِيْعًا وَبَصِيْرًا]، وَضِدُّهُمَا [كَوْنُهُ أَصَمَّ وَكَوْنُهُ أَعْمَى]، وَ الدَّلِيْلُ عَلَى ذلِكَ: دَلِيْلُ السَّمْع وَدَلِيْلُ الْبَصَر

وَ يَجِبُ فِي حَقِّهِ تَعَالَى: [كَوْنُهُ مُتَكَلِّمًا] - وَضِدُّهُ [كَوْنُهُ أَبْكَمَ]، وَ الدَّلِيْلُ عَلَى ذلِكَ: دَلِيْلُ الْكَلَام

وَالْجَائِزُ فِي حَقِّهِ تَعَالَى: [فِعْلُ كُلِّ مُمْكِنٍ أَوْ تَرْكُهُ]، وَالدَّلِيْلُ عَلَى ذلِكَ: أَنَّهُ لَوْ وَجَبَ عَلَيْهِ سبحانه وَتَعَالَى فِعْلُ شَيْءٍ أَوْ تَرْكُهُ لَصَارَ الْجَائِزُ وَاجِبًا أَوْ مُسْتَحِيْلًا وَهُوَ مُحَالٌ

The Matters of Prophethood

النُّبُوَّات

Truthfulness[24] (*al-Sidq*) is necessary for the Messengers ﷺ. The proof for that is, were they to lie, then Allah's report ﷻ [of them being truthful] would have been false, which is impossible. Its opposite is **lying**[25] (*al-kidhb*).

---

24   According to Sunni Islam (*Ahl al-Sunna wa al-Jama'ah*), one trait of the Prophets ﷺ is that they are infallible and do not commit sins. The Qur'an states, *Yusuf! O truthful one! Explain to us [the meaning of] seven fat cattle…* (Yusuf 12:46) and *And mention in the Book, Idris. Indeed, he was a man of truth and a prophet.* (Maryam 19:56)

$$\text{۞} \ldots \text{يُوسُفُ أَيُّهَا الصِّدِّيقُ أَفْتِنَا فِى سَبْعِ بَقَرَاتٍ}$$

(Yusuf 12:46)

$$\text{۞ وَاذْكُرْ فِى الْكِتَابِ إِدْرِيسَ ۚ إِنَّهُ كَانَ صِدِّيقًا نَّبِيًّا}$$

(Maryam 19:56)

25   The disbelieving Quraysh replied to the Prophetic summons to believe in him ﷺ at Mounts Safa and Marwa at the beginning of the public invitation by saying 'we've never experienced lies from you before' (*ma jarrabna minka kadhiban qatt*).

وَيَجِبُ فِي حَقِّ الرُّسُلِ عَلَيْهِمُ الصَّلَاةُ وَالسَّلَامُ:
[اَلصِّدْقُ]، وَضِدُّهُ [اَلْكَذِبُ]، وَ الدَّلِيْلُ عَلَى ذلِكَ:
أَنَّهُمْ لَوْ كَذِبُوْا لَكَانَ خَبَرُ اللهِ سُبْحَانَهُ وَتَعَالَى
كَاذِبًا، وَهُوَ مُحَالٌ

Trustworthiness[26] (*al-Amanah*) is necessary for them ﷺ. The proof for that is were they to commit forbidden (haram) or detestable[27] (makruh) acts, then we would have been ordered to do the same [since we have been commanded to follow them], and it is not valid [i.e. it is absurd] that we are ordered to do something forbidden or detestable. Its opposite is **treachery** (*al-Khiyana*).

---

26   In a display of trustworthiness, the Prophet ﷺ discharged his trust when the would-be assassins plotted an assassination attempt and surrounded his house. The Prophet ﷺ charged Ali ؏ to stay in his stead to oversee the deposits his people left with him because of his trustworthiness while he miraculously exited, walking right between them, reciting the opening verses from Surah Yasin until Allah's Word ... *We have covered them up so they cannot see* and blowing it onto them. (Ibn Hisham)

27   This is taken from a principle in hadith science called 'clarifying permissibility' or bayan al-jawaz. An example of this is in the hadith where once while the Prophet ﷺ was travelling and happened to be performing an optional fast, Hafsa ؏ gave a drink of milk to the Prophet. He partook ﷺ, as scholars explain, to show the permissibility of breaking one's optional fast while travelling.

وَيَجِبُ فِيْ حَقِّهِمْ عَلَيْهِمُ الصَّلَاةُ وَالسَّلَامُ: [اَلْأَمَانَةُ]، وَضِدُّهَا [الْخِيَانَةُ]. وَ الدَّلِيْلُ عَلَى ذَلِكَ: أَنَّهُمْ لَوْ خَانُوْا بِفِعْلٍ مُحَرَّمٍ، أَوْ مَكْرُوهٍ لَكُنَّا مَأْمُوْرِيْنَ بِمِثْلِ ذَلِكَ وَلَا يَصِحُّ أَنْ نُؤْمَرَ بِمُحَرَّمٍ أَوْ مَكْرُوهٍ

Conveying what they were ordered to convey to creation[28] (*Tablighu ma umiru bi tablighi lil khalq*) is necessary for them ﷺ. The proof for that is were they to conceal any part of what they were ordered to convey, then we too would have been ordered to conceal knowledge, and it is not valid [i.e. absurd] that we be ordered to conceal knowledge, because the concealer of knowledge is cursed. Its opposite is **concealing that**[29] (*kitmanu dhalik*).

---

28   The Qur'an states, *It is not upon us but to convey the message clearly* (Yasin 36:17)

$$وَمَا عَلَيْنَا إِلَّا الْبَلَاغُ الْمُبِينُ ۝$$

(Yasin 36:17)

29   The Qur'an states, *Those who conceal the clear signs We have sent down, and the guidance, after We have made it clear for the people in the Book – on them shall be Allah's curse, and the curse of those entitled to curse* (Baqara 2:159). The hadith states, 'Whoever was asked about Sacred knowledge that he possesses but conceals it, then a bridle made of fire will be tied around his mouth on the Day of Resurrection.' (Bukhari)

$$إِنَّ الَّذِينَ يَكْتُمُونَ مَا أَنزَلْنَا مِنَ الْبَيِّنَاتِ وَالْهُدَىٰ مِن بَعْدِ$$
$$مَا بَيَّنَّاهُ لِلنَّاسِ فِي الْكِتَابِ ۙ أُولَٰئِكَ يَلْعَنُهُمُ اللَّهُ وَيَلْعَنُهُمُ$$
$$اللَّاعِنُونَ ۝$$

(Baqara 2:159)

وَيَجِبُ فِي حَقِّهِمْ عَلَيْهِمُ الصَّلَاةُ وَالسَّلَامُ، [تَبْلِيغ
ما أُمِرُوا بِتَبْلِيغِهِ لِلْخَلْقِ]، وَضِدُّهُ [كِتْمَانُ
ذَلِكَ]، وَ الدَّلِيلُ عَلَى ذَلِكَ: أَنَّهُمْ لَوْ كَتَمُوا شَيْئًا
مِمَّا أُمِرُوا بِتَبْلِيغِهِ لَكُنَّا مَأْمُورِينَ بِكِتْمَانِ
الْعِلْمِ، وَلَا يَصِحُّ أَنْ نُؤْمَرَ بِهِ لِأَنَّ كَاتِمَ الْعِلْمِ
مَلْعُونٌ

Astuteness[30] (*al-Fatanah*) is necessary for them ﷺ. The proof for that is were they not astute, they would not have been able to establish a proof against their opponent, which is impossible, because the Qur'an has shown them establishing proofs against their opponents in several instances. Its opposite is **dim-wittedness** (*al-baladah*).

THE POSSIBLE

Any human conditions that do not detract from their high status, such as illness and the like are possible for them ﷺ. The proof for that is witnessing it in them ﷺ.

---

30   The Qur'an recounts that Prophet Ibrahim ﷺ used a rational argument to debate the tyrant Nimrod and silenced his opponent (Baqara 2:258). The enemies of the Messenger of Allah ﷺ would say about him, 'he makes our intelligent look foolish' (*yusaffih ahlamana*) i.e. by invalidating their fallacies with rational proofs.

أَلَمْ تَرَ إِلَى الَّذِى حَاجَّ إِبْرَاهِيمَ فِي رَبِّهِ أَنْ آتَاهُ اللَّهُ الْمُلْكَ إِذْ قَالَ إِبْرَاهِيمُ رَبِّيَ الَّذِى يُحْىِ وَيُمِيتُ قَالَ أَنَا أُحْىِ وَأُمِيتُ قَالَ إِبْرَاهِيمُ فَإِنَّ اللَّهَ يَأْتِى بِالشَّمْسِ مِنَ الْمَشْرِقِ فَأْتِ بِهَا مِنَ الْمَغْرِبِ فَبُهِتَ الَّذِى كَفَرَ وَاللَّهُ لَا يَهْدِى الْقَوْمَ الظَّالِمِينَ ۞

(Baqara 2:258)

42

وَيَجِبُ فِي حَقِّهِمْ عَلَيْهِمُ الصَّلَاةُ وَالسَّلَامُ: [اَلْفَطَانَةُ]، وَضِدُّهَا [اَلْبَلَادَةُ]، وَ الدَّلِيلُ عَلَى ذلِكَ: أَنَّهُ لَوِ انْتَفَتْ عَنْهُمُ الْفَطَانَةُ لَمَا قَدَرُوْا أَنْ يُقِيمُوا حُجَّةً عَلَى الْخَصْمِ وَهُوَ مُحَالٌ، لِأَنَّ الْقُرْآنَ دَلَّ فِيْ مَوَاضِعَ كَثِيْرَةٍ عَلَى إِقَامَتِهِمُ الْحُجَّةَ عَلَى الْخَصْمِ

THE POSSIBLE

وَالْجَائِزُ فِي حَقِّهِمْ عَلَيْهِمُ الصَّلَاةُ وَالسَّلَامُ: [اَلْأَعْرَاضُ الْبَشَرِيَّةُ الَّتِي لَا تُؤَدِّيْ إِلَى نَقْصٍ فِيْ مَرَاتِبِهِمُ الْعَلِيَّةِ]: كَالْمَرَضِ وَنَحْوِهِ، وَ الدَّلِيْلُ عَلَى ذلِكَ: مُشَاهَدَتُهَا بِهِمْ عَلَيْهِمُ الصَّلَاةُ وَالسَّلَامُ

Conclusion

It is necessary to know the Prophet's ﷺ lineage from his father and mother's side. As for his lineage from his father's side, he is our master Muhammad

1. son of 'Abdullah
2. son of 'Abd al-Muttalib
3. son of Hashim
4. son of 'Abd al-Manaf
5. son of Qusayy
6. son of Kilab
7. son of Murrah
8. son of Ka'b
9. son of Lu'ayy
10. son of Ghalib
11. son of Fihr
12. son of Malik
13. son of al-Nadr
14. son of Kinanah
15. son of Khuzaymah
16. son of Mudrikah
17. son of Ilyas
18. son of Mudar
19. son of Nizar
20. son of M'add
21. son of 'Adnan

خَاتِمَةٌ

يَجِبُ عَلَى الشَّخْصِ أَنْ يَعْرِفَ نَسَبَهُ صَلَّى اللهُ عَلَيْهِ وَسَلَّمَ مِنْ جِهَةِ أَبِيهِ، وَمِنْ جِهَةِ أُمِّهِ

أَمَّا نسبه صَلَّى اللهُ عَلَيْهِ وَسَلَّمَ مِنْ جِهَةِ أَبِيهِ: فَهُوَ سَيِّدُنَا مُحَمَّد بْنُ عَبْدِ اللهِ بْنِ عَبْدِ الْمُطَّلِب بْنِ هَاشِم بْنِ عَبْدِ مَنَاف بْنِ قُصَيّ بْنِ كِلَاب بْنِ مُرَّةَ بْنِ كَعْب بْنِ لُؤَيّ بْنِ غَالِب بْنِ فِهْر بْنِ مَالِك بْنِ النَّضْرِ بْنِ كِنَانَة بْنِ خُزَيْمَة بْنِ مُدْرِكَة بْنِ إِلْيَاسَ بْنِ مُضَر بْنِ نِزَارَ بْنِ مَعَدّ بْنِ عَدْنَانَ،

45

And beyond him to Adam 🕮, there is no sound chain of narration.

As for his lineage 🕮 from his mother's side, he is our master Muhammad, son of Aminah, daughter of Wahb, son of 'Abd Manaf, son of Zuhrah, son of Kilab. Then she joins him 🕮 at his forefather, Kilab.

It is also necessary to know that he has a Reservoir (al-Hawd) [in the Hereafter], he 🕮 will intercede in the final judgment, and this [specific] intercession (al-Shafa'ah) is unique to him 🕮.[31]

---

31 There are several categories of people who will intercede for other believers, such as those who memorized the Qur'an, the miscarried baby for its parents, scholars, the Prophet 🕮 himself, and Allah the Exalted.

وَلَيْسَ فِيمَا بَعْدَهُ إِلَى آدَمَ - عَلَيْهِ الصَّلَاةُ
وَالسَّلَامُ - طَرِيقٌ صَحِيحٌ فِيمَا يُنْقَلُ

وَأَمَّا نَسَبُهُ صَلَّى اللهُ عَلَيْهِ وَسَلَّمَ مِنْ جِهَةِ أُمِّهِ
فَهُوَ: سَيِّدُنَا مُحَمَّدُ بْنُ آمِنَةَ بِنْتِ وَهْبٍ بْنِ عَبْدُ
مَنَافٍ بِنْ زُهْرَةَ بْنِ كِلَابٍ، فَتَجْتَمِعُ مَعَهُ صَلَّى
اللهُ عَلَيْهِ وَسَلَّمَ فِيْ جَدِّهِ كِلَاب

وَمِمَّا يَجِبُ أَيْضًا: أَنْ يَعْلَمَ أَنَّ لَهُ حَوْضًا، وَأَنَّهُ
صَلَّى اللهُ عَلَيهِ وَسَلَّمَ يَشْفَعُ فِي فَضْلِ الْقَضَاءِ،
وَهَذِهِ الشَّفَاعَةُ مُخْتَصَّةٌ بِهِ صَلَّى اللهُ عَلَيْهِ وَسَلَّمَ

It is also necessary to know the Messengers explicitly mentioned in the Qur'an. As for the others, it is necessary to know them in general. Someone has versified the prophets that are specifically necessary to know:

> Adam, Idris, Nuh and Hud;
>> Salih, Ibrahim and Lut,
>
> Isma'il, Ishaq, Ya'qub,
>> Handsome Yusuf, patient Ayyub,
>
> Shu'ayb, don't forget Harun,
>> Musa, al-Yasa', Dhu 'l-Kifl, Dawud,
>
> Sulayman, Ilyas, Yunus too,
>> Zakariyya, Yahya, and 'Isa then,
>>> The Best of the Prophets, Muhammad ﷺ[32]

---

32 This translation of this poem has been rearranged to make it rhyme in English in order to facilitate memorization for English readers.

وَمِمَّا يَجِبُ أَيْضًا أَنْ يَعرفهم اَلرُّسُلَ الْمَذْكُورَةِ فِي الْقُرْآنِ تَفْصِيلًا، وَأَمَّا غَيْرُهُمْ فَيَجِبُ عَلَيْهِ أَنْ يَعْرِفَهُمْ إِجْمَالًا، وَقَدْ نَظَمَ بَعْضُهُمُ الْأَنْبِيَاءَ الَّتِي تَجِبُ مَعْرِفَتُهُمْ تَفْصِيلًا، فَقَالَ:

حَتْمٌ عَلَى كُلِّ ذِي التَّكْلِيفِ مَعْرِفَةٌ
بِأَنْبِيَاءٍ عَلَى التَّفْصِيلِ قَدْ عُلِمُوا

فِي تِلْكَ حُجَّتُنَا مِنْهُم ثَمَانِيَةٌ
مِنْ بَعْدِ عَشْرٍ وَيَبْقَى سَبْعَةٌ وَهُمْ

إِدْرِيسُ هُودٌ شُعَيْبٌ صَالِحٌ وَكَذَا
ذُو الْكِفْلِ آدَمُ بِالْمُخْتَارِ قَدْ خُتِمُوا

It is also necessary to believe that his ﷺ generation is the best generation, then the one after it, then the one after that.[33]

An individual should know his children ﷺ. They are, according to the sound position: our master al-Qasim, our lady Zaynab, our lady Ruqayyah, our lady Fatimah, our lady Umm Kulthum, our master 'Abdullah, who was nicknamed the Good and Pure, and our master Ibrahim. All of them are from our lady Khadijah the Great, except our master Ibrahim, who is from Mariyah the Copt.

This is the end of what Allah ﷻ has facilitated through His bounty and generosity. All praise is due to Allah, Lord of the worlds; and may Allah's blessings and peace be upon our master Muhammad, his family, and his companions.

---

33   It is stated in hadith, 'The best of generations is my generation; then those after them, then those after them.' (Bukhari)

مِمَّا يَجِبُ إِعْتِقَادُهُ أَيْضًا أَنَّ قَرْنَهُ أَفْضَلُ الْقُرُوْنِ،
ثُمَّ الْقَرْنُ الَّذِي بَعْدَهُ، ثُمَّ الْقَرْنُ الَّذِي بَعْدَهُ

وَيَنْبَغِي لِلشَّخْصِ أَنْ يَعْرِفَ أَوْلَادَهُ صَلَّى اللهُ
عَلَيْهِ وَسَلَّمَ وَهُمْ عَلَى الصَّحِيْحِ: سَيِّدُنَا الْقَاسِمُ،
وَسَيِّدَتُنَا زَيْنَبُ، وَسَيِّدَتُنَا رُقَيَّةُ، وَسَيِّدَتُنَا فَاطِمَةُ،
وَسَيِّدَتُنَا أُمُّ كُلْثُوْم، وَسَيِّدُنَا عَبْدُ اللهِ وَهُوَ
المُلَقَّبُ بِالطَّيِّبِ وَالطَّاهِرِ، وَسَيِّدُنَا إِبْرَاهِيْمُ،
وَكُلُّهُمْ مِنْ سَيِّدَتِنَا خَدِيْجَةَ الْكُبْرَى، إِلَّا إِبْرَاهِيْمُ
فَمِنْ مَارِيَةَ الْقِبْطِيَّة

وَهَذَا آخِرُ مَا يَسَّرَهُ اللهُ مِنْ فَضْلِهِ وَكَرَمِهِ،
وَالْحَمْدُ اللهِ رَبِّ الْعَالَمَين، وَصَلَّى اللهُ عَلَى سَيِّدِنَا
محمد وَ عَلَى آلِهِ وَصَحْبِهِ وَسَلَّم

Appendix

NECESSARY	IMPOSSIBLE

SIFAH NAFSIYYAH

Existence	اَلْوُجُوْدُ	Non-existence	اَلْعَدَمُ

SIFAH SALBIYYAH

Beginninglessness	اَلْقِدَمُ	Contingency	اَلْحُدُوْثُ
Endlessness	اَلْبَقَاءُ	Transience	اَلْفَنَاءُ
Difference from originated things	اَلْمُخَالَفَةُ لِلْحَوَادِثِ	Likeness	اَلْمُمَاثَلَةُ
Self-Subsistence	اَلْقِيَامُ بِالنَّفْسِ	Requiring a determinant	اَلْاِحْتِيَاجُ إِلَى الْمَحَلِّ وَالْمُخَصِّصِ
Oneness	اَلْوَحْدَانِيَّةُ	Multiplicity	اَلتَّعَدُّدُ

SIFAH AL-MAʾANI

Ability	اَلْقُدْرَةُ	Inability	اَلْعَجْزُ
Will	اَلْإِرَادَةُ	Compulsion	اَلْكَرَاهَةُ
Knowledge	اَلْعِلْمُ	Ignorance	اَلْجَهْلُ
Life	اَلْحَيَاةُ	Death	اَلْمَوْتُ
Hearing	اَلسَّمْعُ	Deafness	اَلصَّمَمُ
Sight	اَلْبَصَرُ	Blindness	اَلْعَمَى
Speech	اَلْكَلَامُ	Muteness	اَلْبُكْمُ

SIFAH AL-MAʾNAWIYYA

His being All-Powerful	كَوْنُهُ قَادِرًا	His being unable	كَوْنُهُ عَاجِزًا
His being Willing	كَوْنُهُ مُرِيْدًا	His being compelled	كَوْنُهُ كَارِهًا
His being All-Knowing	كَوْنُهُ عَالِمًا	His being ignorant	كَوْنُهُ جَاهِلًا
His being Living	كَوْنُهُ حَيًّا	His being dead	كَوْنُهُ مَيِّتًا
His being All-Hearing	كَوْنُهُ سَمِيْعًا	His being deaf	كَوْنُهُ أَصَمُّ
His being All-Seeing	كَوْنُهُ بَصِيْرًا	His Being blind	أَعْمَى كَوْنُهُ

THE POSSIBLE

Doing or leaving anything possible   فِعْلُ كُلِّ مُمْكِنٍ أَوْ تَرْكُهُ

ATTRIBUTES OF THE PROPHETS

NECESSARY		IMPOSSIBLE	
Truthfulness	اَلصِّدْقُ	Lying	اَلْكِذْبُ
Loyalty	اَلْأَمَانَةُ	Treachery	اَلْخِيَانَةُ
Conveying what they were ordered to convey to creation	تَبْلِيغُ مَا أُمِرُوْا بِتَبْلِيغِهِ لِلْخَلْقِ	Concealing that	كِتْمَانُ ذَلِكَ
Astuteness	اَلْفَطَانَةُ	Stupidity	اَلْبَلَادَةُ

THE POSSIBLE

Human conditions that do not detract from their high status   اَلْأَعْرَاضُ الْبَشَرِيَّةُ الَّتِي لَا تُؤَدِّى إِلَى نَقْصٍ فِيْ مَرَاتِبِهِمُ الْعَلِيَّةِ

25 PROPHETS MENTIONED IN THE QUR'AN ﷺ

#	ENGLISH	ARABIC	FEATURES
1	Adam	آدَم	First man First Prophet

2	Idris	إِدْرِيْس	First to write with a pen
3	Nuh	نُوْح	Called to Allah over 950 years
4	Hud	هُوْد	Sent to the people of 'Ad Carved buildings into rock People destroyed with a violent gale
5	Salih	صَالِح	Sent to the people of Thamud Miracle of the she-camel
6	Ibrahim	إِبْرَاهِيْم	Patriarch of the Prophets Father of the Jews and Arabs
7	Lut	لُوْط	Nephew of Ibrahim ﷺ Fled Sodom and Gomorra First migrant for the sake of Allah
8	Ismail	إِسْمَاعِيْل	The sacrifice of Allah Helped re-build the Ka'bah Father of the Arabs
9	Ishaq	إِسْحَاق	Father of the Jews
10	Ya'qub	يَعْقُوْب	Had 12 children which later became the 12 tribes of Israel
11	Yusuf	يُوْسُف	Given half of all beauty Miracle of dream interpretation
12	Ayyub	أَيُّوْب	Paragon of patience
13	Shu'ayb	شُعَيْب	Lived in Madyan
14	Harun	هَارُوْن	Minister for his brother
15	Musa	مُوْسَى	Allah spoke to him directly Parted the Red Sea Received the sacred Tablet
16	al-Yasa'	أَلْيَسَع	Mentioned in the Qur'an
17	Dhu l-Kifl	ذُو الْكِفْل	Mentioned in the Qur'an

18	Dawud	دَاوُد	King Prophet Metal was made malleable for him
19	Sulayman	سُلَيْمَان	King Prophet Controlled the wind, animals, men and jinn
20	Ilyas	إِلْيَاس	Mentioned in the Qur'an
21	Yunus	يُوْنُس	Swallowed by the whale Saved by a special dua Over 100,000 of his people believed in him
22	Zakariyya	زَكَرِيَّا	Cared for Maryam ﷺ His wife was barren when he had his son, Prophet Yahya ﷺ
23	Yahya	يَحْى	Maternal cousin of Jesus ﷺ
24	'Isa	عِيْسى	Miraculously conceived Will return at the end of time Will follow the Sacred Law of Islam
25	Muhammad	مُحَمَّد	Last and final Prophet Greatest Prophet

HIS LINEAGE FROM HIS FATHER'S SIDE ﷺ

#	ARABIC	NAME
1	مُحَمَّد بن	Muhammad son of
2	عَبْد اللهِ بن	'Abdullah son of
3	عَبْدُ الْمُطَّلِبِ بن	'Abdul-Muttalib son of
4	هَاشِم ابن	Hashim son of
5	عَبْد مَنَافِ بن	'Abdul-Manaf son of

6	قُصَيّ بن	Qusayy son of
7	كِلَاب بن	Kilab son of
8	مُرَّة بن	Murrah son of
9	كَعْب بن	Ka'ab son of
10	لُؤَىّ بن	Lu'ayy son of
11	غَالِب بن	Ghalib son of
12	فِهْر بن	Fihr son of
13	مَالِك بن	Malik son of
14	اَلنَّضَر بن	Nadar son of
15	كِنَانة بن	Kinanah son of
16	خُزَيْمَة بن	Khuzaymah son of
17	مُدْرِكَة بن	Mudrikah son of
18	إِلْيَاس بن	Ilyas son of
19	مُضَر بن	Mudar son of
20	نِزَار بن	Nizar son of
21	مَعَدّ بن	Ma'add son of
22	عَدْنَان	'Adnan

WIVES OF THE MESSENGER ﷺ

#	ARABIC	NAME
1	خَدِيْجَةُ بِنْت خُوَيْلِد	Khadijah bint Khuwaylid

2	عَائِشَةُ بِنْت اَبِى بَكْرٍ الصِّدِيْق	'Aishah bint Abi Bakr as-Siddiq
3	حَفْصَةُ بِنْت عُمَرِ ابْنَ الْخَطَّاب	Hafsah bint 'Umar ibn al-Khattab
4	اُمْ حَبِيْبَة بِنْت اَبِى سُفْيَان	Umm Habiba bint Abi Sufyan
5	اُمْ سَلَمَة بِنْت اُمَيَّة	Umm Salama bint Umayyah
6	سَوْدَةُ بِنْت زُمْعَة بِنْ قَيْس	Sawdah bint Zum'ah bin Qays
7	زَيْنَبُ بِنْت جَحْش	Zaynab bint Jahsh
8	مَيْمُوْنَه بِنْت الْحَارِث الْهِلاَلِيَّة	Maymuna bint al-Harith al-Hilaliyah
9	زَيْنَبُ بِنْت خُزَيْمَة الْهِلاَلِيَّة	Zaynab bint Khuzaimah al-Hilaliyah
10	جُوَيْرِيَّة بِنْت الْحَارِث	Juwayriyah bint al-Harith
11	صَفِيَّه بِنْت حَيّ بِنْ اَخْطَب مِنْ بَنِى النَّضِيْر	Safiyyah bint Hayy ibn Akhtab from Bani Nadir

CHILDREN OF THE MESSENGER ﷺ

Note: All of his children ﷺ are from Khadija ؆ except Ibrahim, who is from Mariya.

#	ARABIC	NAME
1	سَيِّدُنَا الْقَاسِم	Our master al-Qasim
2	سَيِّدَتُنَا زَيْنَب	Our lady Zaynab
3	سَيِّدَتُنَا رُقَيَّة	Our lady Ruqayyah

59

4	سَيِّدَتُنَا فَاطِمَة	Our lady Fatima
5	سَيِّدَتُنَا أُمْ كُلْثُوْم	Our lady Umm Kulthum
6	سَيِّدُنَا عَبْدُ اللهِ وَهُوَ الْمُلَقَّبُ بِالطَّيِّبِ وَالطَّاهِرِ	Our master 'Abdullah also known as Tayyib and Tahir
7	سَيِّدُنَا إِبراهيم	Our master Ibrahim

THE LEVELS OF HEAVEN & HELL

NAME	LEVELS OF JANNAH	NAME	LEVELS OF JAHANNAM
اَلْفِرْدَوْس	al-Firdous	جَهَنَّم	Jahannam
اَلْمَقَامَة	al-Muqamah	اَلسَّعِيْر	al-Sa'ir
دَارُ الْقَرَارِ	Dar al-Qarar	سَقَر	Saqar
دَارُ السَّلاَم	Dar al-Salam	جَحِيْم	Jahim
اَلْمَأْوى	al-Ma'wa	حُطَمَة	Hutamah
اَلنَّعِيْمُ	al-Na'im	ذَاتَ اللَّهَب	Dhat al-Lahab
اَلْخُلْد	al-Khuld	حَاوِيَة	Hawiyah
اَلْعَدْن	al-'Adan	لَظى	Ladhaw

Acknowledgments

Bismillah, Alhamdulilah, was salatu was salamu ʿala Rasulillah, wa ʿala Alihi wa sahbihi wa sallam. To Shaykh Ahmed Saad al-Azhari for his patience, knowledge and beautiful teaching style. Thank you for connecting me to the author, Shaykh al-Islam, and transmitting this important beginner's text. To Shaykh Faraz Rabbani for his guidance and assistance. To Ustadh Abdul Aziz Suraqah for his aid, brotherhood, and advice in translation. To Ustadh Abdus Shakur Brooks, my brother, teacher, and friend, with whom I studied this book for the second time in 2014 CE. May Allah bless you in all your endeavors.

To Maulvi Muhammad Yusuf who first introduced me to ʿilm al-kalam or Islamic theology, and this book in 2004 CE. To Mohammed Shehata for procuring the original picture of Imam al-Bajuri from Masjid al-Azhar. To Shuaiyb Newton and Isa Bey, thank you brothers for the perspective and editing session. And last, but not least, to Imam Zameer Sattaur, Adnaan Sattaur, and the Imam Ghazali Institute (along with their team) for bringing this book to fruition. May Allah bless my beautiful city of Toronto and may He grant us, and all who study this, the true knowledge and experience of Allah taʿala that prevents us from sins and the tawfiq to do good works, by the rank of His Mustafa ﷺ. And our final word is that all praise belongs to Allah, Lord of the worlds.

About the IGI Essentials Series

Without a doubt, the Islamic tradition is one that is deep and vast. It is one that is filled with an ocean of jewels. As Muslims living in the West, we have found ourselves often playing an important role in recent times: to preserve and protect our inherited tradition, while firmly establishing it for generations to come.

The uniqueness of the Islamic tradition is one where each successive generation of scholars have received their knowledge from a verifiable chain of transmission. This has allowed Muslims in every generation the ability to trace the source. The Imam Ghazali Institute has been conducting Islamic education intensives of varying lengths since 2007 with the goal of reviving love and attachment to the traditional sciences of sacred knowledge.

The IGI Essentials series aims to introduce English-speaking students around the globe to a text-based study of what are the core essentials a believer would need to know in: Aqidah, Hadith, Fiqh, Tasawwuf, Sirah, and Tafsir. It is our hope that a student will go beyond a simple read of the text and seek out a teacher with whom they can study it with, inshaAllah.

For more information about the Imam Ghazali Institute, please visit www.imamghazali.org.

NOTES

NOTES

THIS PAGE INTENTIONALLY LEFT BLANK

THIS PAGE INTENTIONALLY LEFT BLANK

THIS PAGE INTENTIONALLY LEFT BLANK